NATURAL WONDERS

The Amazon Rain Forest

The Largest Rain Forest in the World

Galadriel Watson

WEIGL PUBLISHERS INC.

Published by Weigl Publishers Inc.
350 5ᵗʰ Avenue, Suite 3304, PMB 6G
New York, NY 10118-0069
USA

Web site: www.weigl.com

Library of Congress Cataloging-in-Publication Data

Watson, Galadriel Findlay.
  The Amazon rain forest : the largest rain forest in the world /
by Galadriel Watson.
      p. cm. — (Natural wonders)
  Includes index.
  ISBN 1-59036-270-5 (lib. bdg. : alk. paper) 1-59036-276-4 (pbk.)
  1. Rain forests—Amazon River Region—Juvenile literature.
I. Title. II. Natural wonders (Weigl Publishers)
  QH112.W38 2004
  918.1'1—dc22
                          2004013604

Printed in the United States of America
1 2 3 4 5 6 7 8 9 0   08 07 06 05 04

Editorial Services
BookMark Publishing, Inc.

Editor
Heather C. Hudak

Design
Terry Paulhus

Layout
Biner Design

Photo Researcher
Dawn Friedman,
BookMark Publishing, Inc.

Photo Description
*Cover: Emergent treetops rise above
the canopy of the Amazon rain forest.*
*Title page: Some of the largest water
lilies in the world are found in the
Amazon rain forest.*

Photograph Credits

Every reasonable effort has been made to trace ownership and to obtain
permission to reprint copyright material. The publishers would be pleased
to have any errors or omissions brought to their attention so that they may
be corrected in subsequent printings.

Cover: The Amazon rain forest (Galen Rowell/CORBIS/MAGMA);
CORBIS/MAGMA: pages 11 (Collart Herve/Corbis Sygma), 14
(Danny Lehman); **Corel Corporation:** pages 13, 28; **The Granger
Collection, New York:** page 15; **Wolfgang Kaehler 2004,
www.wkaehlerphoto.com:** pages 1, 8, 10, 18, 21, 22, 24, 27B; **Photo
Researchers, Inc:** pages 4 (Gregory G. Dimijian), 6 (Martin Wendler),
12 (David M. Schleser/Nature's Images), 19 (Alison Wright), 20 (Victor
Englebert), 26B (David R. Frazier Photolibrary); **Photos.com:** pages
23T, 23B, 26T, 27T; **Visuals Unlimited:** page 25 (Pegasus).

Contents

A Wealth of Life

With an area of more than 2 million square miles (5.2 million square kilometers), the Amazon rain forest in South America is the largest rain forest in the world. It is so large that it covers an area equal to about half of the United States.

A wealth of plants and animals live in this vast region. In fact, more **species** of plants and animals live in the Amazon rain forest than in any other place on Earth. Fruits, nuts, coffee, and other foods are farmed in the Amazon. Certain plants are used to make important medicines. Thousands of types of monkeys, birds, insects, and other animals thrive in the rain forest's hot, wet climate.

■ **Scientists believe the rain forest is home to thousands of plant and animal species that have not yet been identified.**

Amazon Rain Forest Facts

- Temperatures in the Amazon rain forest average about 80° Fahrenheit (27° Celsius), with up to 90 percent humidity. To humans, this feels like a steam bath.

- The Amazon region receives about 9 feet (2.7 meters) of rainfall a year. By comparison, the average U.S. city receives less than 3 feet (0.9 m) per year.

- The Amazon rain forest covers about one-third of the continent of South America.

- The rain forest surrounds the Amazon River, the second-longest river in the world. The Nile In Africa Is the longest river in the world.

- The Amazon River carries 16 percent of all the water on Earth.

- The equator runs across the northern portion of the Amazon rain forest. Almost all of the world's tropical rain forests are located on or near the equator.

The Amazon Rain Forest Locator

Where in the World?

The Amazon rain forest is home to the 4,000-mile (6,437-km) Amazon River. It runs from the Andes Mountains to the Atlantic Ocean on the east coast of South America. Along the way, more than 1,000 **tributaries** feed into the Amazon. When the warm season arrives in the Andes, mountain snowmelt runs down to the Amazon. The already huge river swells and floods.

The Amazon rain forest surrounds the river. Much of the region is wild jungle, and few cities exist there. Part of the rain forest sits in the Tumucumaque Mountains National Park in Brazil. This protected area is the largest tropical forest national park in the world.

■ **The twisting, winding route of the Amazon River crosses nine different South American countries.**

Puzzler

Most of the Amazon rain forest lies in the country of Brazil, but it also extends into eight other countries.

Q Where are these countries located? Find each one on the map.

Bolivia
Brazil
Colombia
Ecuador
French Guiana
Guyana
Peru
Suriname
Venezuela

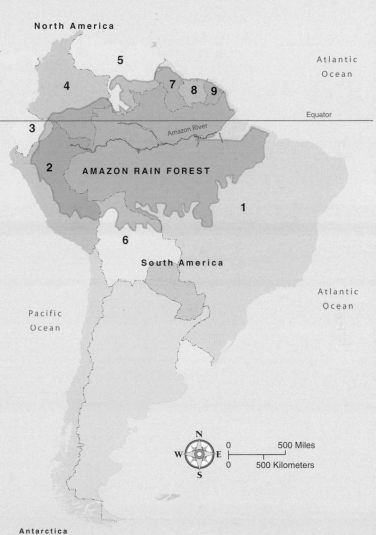

North America

Atlantic Ocean

Equator

Amazon River

AMAZON RAIN FOREST

South America

Atlantic Ocean

Pacific Ocean

Antarctica

500 Miles
500 Kilometers

A 1. Brazil 2. Peru 3. Ecuador 4. Colombia 5. Venezuela 6. Bolivia 7. Guyana 8. Suriname 9. French Guiana

A Trip Back in Time

Millions of years ago, before humans lived on Earth, the Amazon River flowed west into the Pacific Ocean. Later, the region's tectonic plates, the rigid pieces of land that make up Earth's outer shell, began to shift. The tectonic shift pushed up huge masses of rock to form the Andes Mountains. With the mountains in its path, the Amazon River gradually found a new route. Eventually, the river moved east and reached the Atlantic Ocean. This occurred about 8 million years ago.

In some parts of the world, such as North America, **ice age** glaciers covered the land and killed most living things. The Amazon, however, has never been covered by glaciers. This has allowed Amazon plant and animal species to develop uninterrupted for millions of years.

▬ Like the rain forest, many Amazon trees are very old. Some ceiba trees have been known to live for more than two centuries.

Rain Forest Layers

The rain forest is divided into several layers, each with very different living conditions.

Emergents: Gigantic treetops rise above the rest of the forest's trees. Mostly birds and insects live here. This layer receives more sunlight than other layers.

Canopy: The treetops reach up to 165 feet (50 m). This area traps the most water and sunlight. These treetops produce the most food for the forest's creatures.

Understory: Here live shrubs and shorter, younger trees that reach to about 60 feet (18 m). Only about 2 percent of sunlight reaches the understory.

Floor: The floor is dark. Only 0–2 percent of sunlight and very little water reach the floor. Few plants can grow in this darkness. The ground is covered with a layer of decomposing leaves and other matter called **humus**. Many fungi and insects live on the floor layer.

Plentiful Plants

Only a small amount of light and water reach the floor of the rain forest, so the soil is too poor to allow many plants to grow in the ground. In other environments, plants draw **nutrients** from the soil, but rain forest plants keep most nutrients in their leaves and tissues. They also receive nutrients from the floor's layer of humus.

Despite the poor soil, the Amazon rain forest holds countless types of plants. There are more than 2,500 species of trees. Many other plants make their homes in these trees. Lianas—thick, woody vines—connect to young trees in the understory. They grow upward and attach themselves to taller branches. Some lianas grow as high as the canopy.

▬ **Epiphytes, also called "air plants," do not have roots in the soil. They live above ground, attached to other plants. They do not feed off their host plant, but rather draw nutrients from air and rain.**

The Rainy Season

The rain forest has just two seasons: a rainy season and a dry season. The rainy season in the Amazon lasts about 4 months. There is still plenty of sunshine, but the clouds take every opportunity to release huge amounts of water. Also during the rainy season, water from snow melting in the Andes runs down the mountains and flows into rivers and streams. Together, the rain and melted snow make for massive flooding in the rain forest. Vast areas of the forest floor are covered in water. Animals either climb trees or scramble to seek higher ground.

The dry season of the Amazon is still quite wet, but the rain is far less frequent. The floodwaters recede, allowing animals to return to the flooded land.

■ Rainy-season downpours can be so heavy that 1 or 2 inches (2.5 to 5 centimeters) of rain can fall in just 1 hour.

Amazon Animals

Some incredible creatures live in the Amazon rain forest. Animals must be on guard against the anaconda, a huge water snake that kills its prey by wrapping its body around the other animal and squeezing it to death. One of the largest spiders in the world, the 10-inch (25-cm) bird-eating spider, lives in the Amazon, too. There are also many mammals, such as sloths, monkeys, and the vampire bat.

Scientists may never know exactly how many animals live in the Amazon. They estimate that there are 1,500 bird species, 3,000 fish species, and 500 mammal species. Rain forest scientists often identify animal species that have never been known to humans. Since 1990, more than a dozen new monkey species have been found in the Amazon region.

■ The leaf-mimic katydid is one of 30 million insect species that live in the Amazon rain forest.

Endangered Species

Some scientists estimate that every day in rain forests, about 100 plant and animal species become extinct. This means if the last member of the species dies, the species will never return to life again. Plant and animal extinction is caused by many different factors that change the rain forest ecosystem. Some causes are natural, and others are caused by humans.

The Amazon's jaguar population is currently in danger. Local ranchers kill jaguars if they suspect the cats have been attacking their herds. Hunters also kill jaguars for their fur.

A threatened plant species is the mahogany tree. People around the world love furniture made of the dark reddish-brown mahogany wood. The trees are cut down so frequently that mahogany might soon become extinct in the Amazon.

■ The jaguar makes its home in the trees of the rain forest. When trees are cut down, the jaguar's habitat is destroyed.

Researching the Forest

The Amazon rain forest canopy holds many mysteries. Since the canopy is so hard to reach, scientists have studied it less than the ocean floor.

In the 1800s, European explorers hired **indigenous** peoples to climb the trees and bring down samples of plant life. Presently, scientists can measure trees using **lasers**. They also use **satellite** pictures to study large areas of the forest.

In recent years, scientists have built platforms high in the trees so they can get a closeup look at canopy life. One scientist even developed a canopy "raft"— a large platform that floats in the air, held up by helium-filled tubes.

Walkways allow people to travel through the canopy of the rain forest on foot. Walkways lead to platforms, where people can stay for hours, or even camp for days.

Biography

Henry Walter Bates (1825–1892)

Henry Walter Bates spent more than a decade studying nature in the Amazon rain forest. Bates was a naturalist, a scientist who studies nature. He was the first person to identify about 7,000 rain forest insects. Bates described his findings in his book, *The Naturalist on the River Amazons*, published in 1863.

Bates was well known for his studies on insect mimicry. Mimicry is when a species of animals looks like another species so that **predators** cannot easily see the animal. For example, the viceroy butterfly, which is eaten by birds, looks like the monarch butterfly, which birds hate to eat. Since the viceroy looks like the monarch, birds often leave the viceroy alone. This animal trait is called "Batesian mimicry," named after Bates.

Facts of Life

Born: February 8, 1825

Hometown: Leicester, England

Occupation: Naturalist

Died: February 16, 1892

The Big Picture

The Amazon rain forest is one of several rain forests in the world. The largest rain forests are in Central and South America, Asia, and Africa. Although these forests cover only about 7 percent of Earth's land, they are home to more than 50 percent of its plant and animal species.

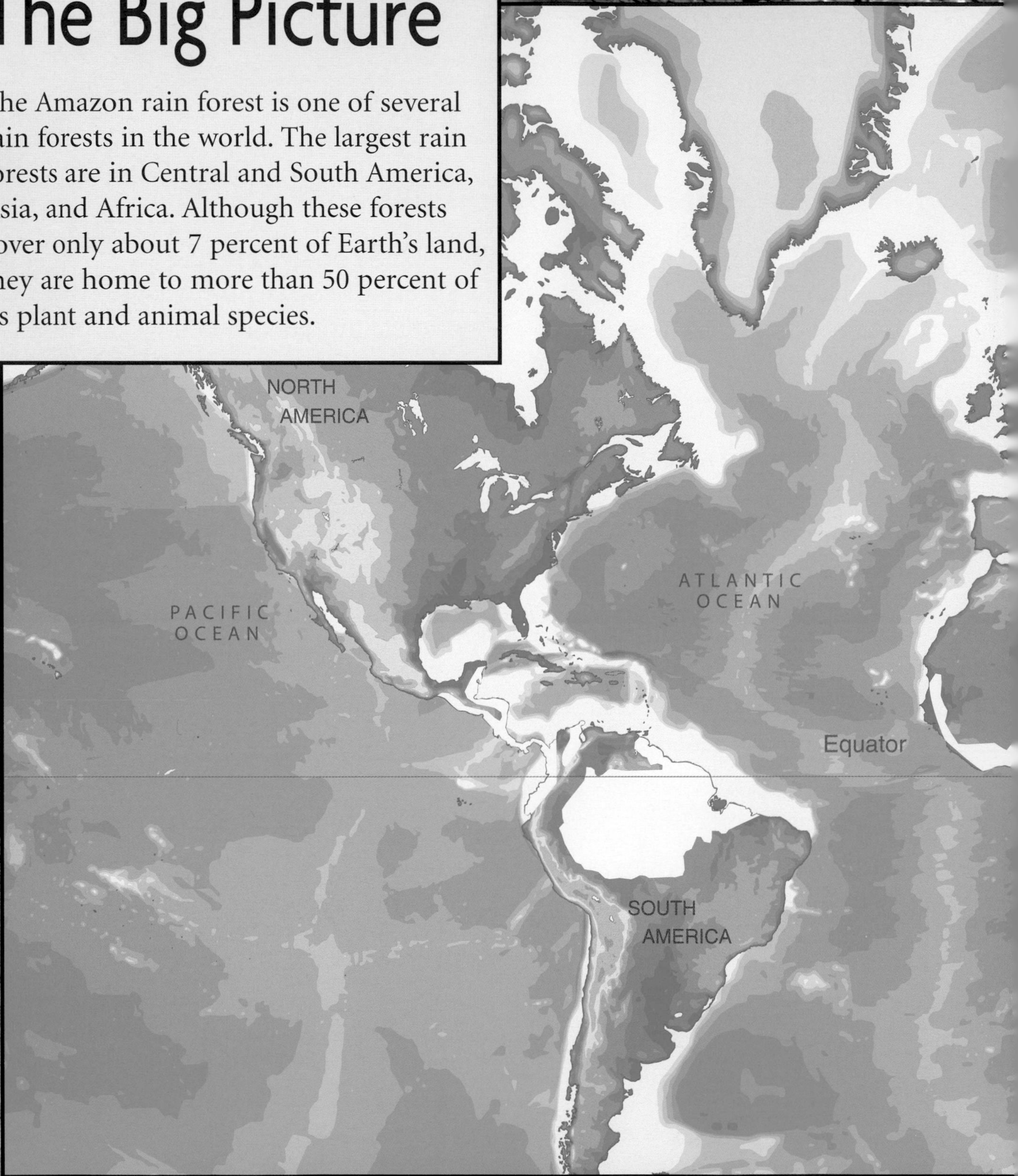

NORTH
AMERICA

PACIFIC
OCEAN

ATLANTIC
OCEAN

Equator

SOUTH
AMERICA

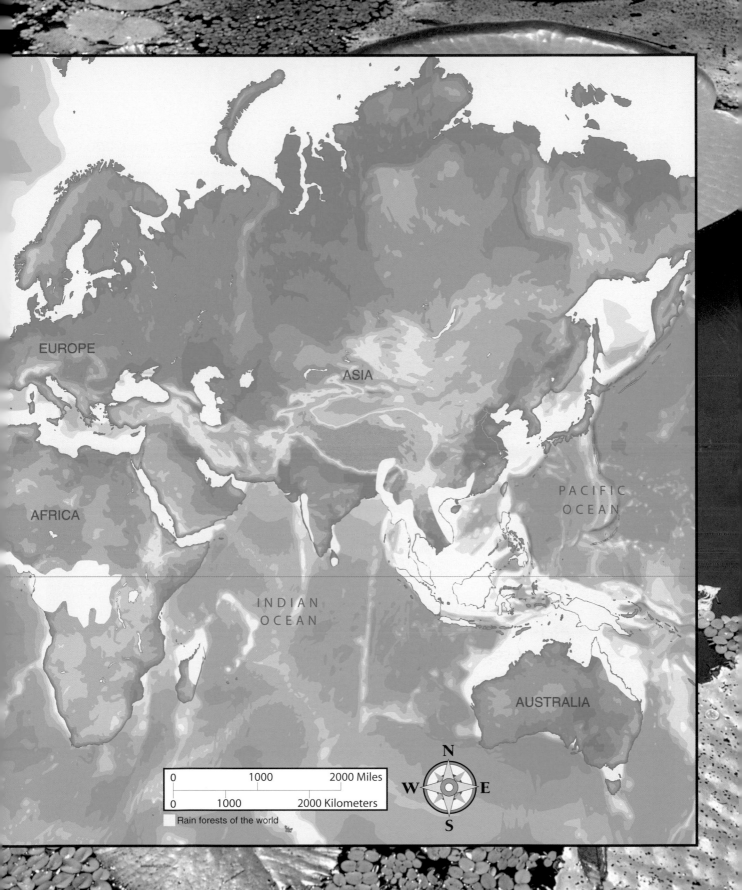

EUROPE

ASIA

AFRICA

PACIFIC
OCEAN

INDIAN
OCEAN

AUSTRALIA

| 0 | | 1000 | | 2000 Miles |
| 0 | | 1000 | | 2000 Kilometers |

N
W E
S

Rain forests of the world

People of the Amazon

The first people to live in the Amazon arrived thousands of years ago. When Spanish conquerors called conquistadors arrived in the 1500s, they destroyed many of these ancient civilizations.

Today, about 30 million people live in the Amazon region. More than half of these people live in cities. Some people live in the city of Manaus, Brazil. Many others are farmers or gold prospectors. Only about 500,000 are indigenous peoples. They belong to about 150 ethnic groups, such as the Yanomami, the Xikrin, and the Juruna.

Amazon rain forest families build their homes on stilts so they can stay above water during the rainy season.

Puzzler

Since the Amazon rain forest is crisscrossed with waterways, and because so much of it floods during the rainy season, the best way to travel is by boat.

Q From what material are the Amazon canoes called *pirogues* made?

A These boats are made from hollowed tree trunks.

Natural Attractions

Tourists who visit the Amazon rain forest are vital to its survival for many reasons. Perhaps most importantly, tourism brings money to people who have little. Visitors spend money on hotels, food, and local products. Also, tourism encourages the local inhabitants to properly care for the wilderness so it will continue to attract visitors. Some hotels have built walkways and platforms to allow tourists to observe the canopy ecosystem as closeup as scientists.

The vast rain forest offers visitors many different opportunities for exploration. Some people travel to the Meeting of the Waters, a place where the dark and light waters of two rivers run side-by-side without mixing. Others visit Lake Janauari Ecological Park to see giant water lilies, measuring up to 7 feet (2.1 m) across.

■ **Tour companies lead visitors on boat tours through the rain forest. Tourists can also hire guides to take them hiking through parts of the forest floor.**

Be Prepared

A visit to the Amazon rain forest can be a rough and rugged trip, but with proper preparation, it can be safe, fascinating, and the experience of a lifetime.

It is important to dress for very hot temperatures and high humidity. Loose-fitting cotton clothing is best.

If traveling on foot through the forest floor, some tour companies recommend bringing "mud shoes," an old pair of inexpensive sneakers.

Many areas of the forest floor receive little sunlight even during daytime, so a flashlight will help in the dark.

Since most of the animals reside high in the canopy, a pair of binoculars is the best way to see them.

A rain forest visit will not be spent entirely in the shade. Be prepared for sunny spots by bringing sunscreen, a hat, and sunglasses.

Be sure to bring insect repellent.

Heavy rains can occur at any time, so a good raincoat or poncho is needed.

Visitors should always have a camera ready. Tourists cannot take plants or animals home from the rain forest, but they can take as many pictures as they want.

The Disappearing Forest

The Amazon rain forest is disappearing at an alarming rate. In 2002, an estimated 10,000 square miles (25,900 sq km) of rain forest were cut or burned just in Brazil. This area is about the same size as the state of Massachusetts. **Deforestation** is a difficult issue because there are both good and bad reasons to clear trees. For instance, the wood from these trees makes products such as furniture and flooring. This brings money into the area economies. On the other hand, deforestation destroys some animals' habitats.

▬ Rain forest trees are cleared to make way for new farms, ranches, roads, mines, and many other uses.

Government and businesses try to replace some of the deforested areas. However the ecosystems that grow in these newer forests contain fewer plants and animal species. Once an ancient rain forest area is cleared, it is likely gone forever.

Should trees be cut down in the Amazon rain forest?

YES	NO
The world's population is increasing and needs wood for fuel and timber.	Countless plant and animal species are wiped out by deforestation.
Selling rain forest trees brings much-needed income into the region.	Indigenous peoples lose their homes and eventually forget important knowledge about the land, its species, and its history.
Land needs to be cleared to build new settlements so people can move out of overcrowded cities.	The loss of trees causes local air temperatures to rise, reduces the amount of rain in the area, and increases the level of **carbon dioxide** in the atmosphere. These factors all contribute to the **greenhouse effect**.

Time Line

90 million years ago
The Andes Mountains begin to form.

30 million years ago
The Amazon River is cut off from the Pacific Ocean.

8 million years ago
The Amazon River breaks through to the Atlantic Ocean.

10–15,000 years ago
The Amazon's earliest inhabitants arrive.

1500s
European explorers first arrive in the Amazon.

1500s
The Spanish conquistadors destroy entire indigenous civilizations.

1541
Europeans complete their first trip down the entire length of the Amazon River.

The toucan is one of the thousands of birds in the Amazon. One-third of the world's bird species lives there.

Manaus, Brazil, is one of the major cities in the Amazon rain forest region.

1740s
Europeans in the Amazon discover **latex**, which becomes a key substance in producing rubber and plastic products.

1825
Henry Walter Bates is born.

1848
Henry Walter Bates first travels to the Amazon.

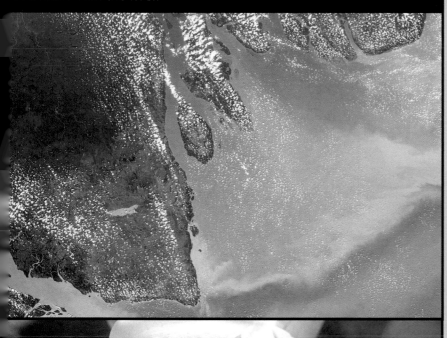

A satellite photo shows the Amazon River feeding into the Atlantic Ocean. The green patches are forest, and the brown area is muddy sediment from the river.

The Amazon rain forest is well known for many spectacular types of orchids.

1863
Henry Walter Bates publishes his book *The Naturalist on the River Amazons*.

1892
Henry Walter Bates dies.

1950
The world's rain forests cover about 8,700,000 square miles (22,532,896 sq km).

1958
Researchers build the first rain forest observation tower in Uganda.

1960s
Researchers build the first suspended walkways in the rain forest.

1970s
Researchers use mountain-climbing equipment to pull themselves up to the canopy.

1980s
After studying insect life in the Amazon rain forest, one researcher determines there are up to 30 million insect species in the world.

1989
The canopy raft is invented.

2002
Brazil's portion of the Amazon loses 10,000 square miles (25,900 sq km) to deforestation.

2002
The Brazilian government announces the creation of Tumucumaque Mountains National Park.

What Have You Learned?

True or False?

Decide whether the following statements are true or false. If the statement is false, make it true.

1. Henry Walter Bates was a conquistador.

2. According to legend, manioc is named after a boy named Mani.

3. People know much more about the rain forest canopy than the ocean floor.

4. The Amazon's jaguar population is increasing.

5. Humus is made partly of decomposing leaves.

ANSWERS

1. False. He was a naturalist.
2. True
3. False. They know less about the canopy.
4. False. The jaguar population is decreasing.
5. True

Short Answer

Answer the following questions using information from the book.

1. To what ocean does the Amazon River flow?

2. What did not cover the Amazon during an ice age?

3. What are the names of the rain forest's layers?

4. What kind of plant does not need soil?

5. What drink has more caffeine than coffee?

ANSWERS
1. The Atlantic Ocean
2. Glaciers
3. Emergents, Canopy, Understory, Floor
4. An epiphyte, or "air plant"
5. Guaraná

Multiple Choice

Choose the best answer for the following questions.

1. The Amazon rain forest is mostly in:
   a) Mexico
   b) Brazil
   c) Ecuador
   d) Argentina

2. Pirogues are a type of:
   a) Food
   b) Flower
   c) Fish
   d) Boat

3. What group of indigenous peoples lives in the Amazon?
   a) The Yanomami
   b) The San
   c) The Aztecs
   d) The Mohawks

4. What do doctors use as a treatment for malaria?
   a) Brazil nut
   b) guaraná
   c) curare
   d) quinine

ANSWERS
1. b
2. d
3. a
4. d

Find Out for Yourself

Books

Barter, James. *The Amazon.* San Diego: Lucent Books, 2003.

Capelas, Afonso Jr. *Amazonia: The Land, the Wildlife, the River, the People.* Toronto: Firefly Books, 2003.

Cheshire, Gerard. *The Tropical Rainforest.* New York: Crabtree Publishing Company, 2001.

Web Sites

Use the Internet to find out more about the people, plants, animals, and geology of the Amazon rain forest.

Journey into Amazonia
www.pbs.org/journeyintoamazonia/enter.html
This site from the Public Broadcast System site gives a great deal of information about the Amazon's flora and fauna.

Amazon Interactive
www.eduweb.com/amazon.html
On this site learn about the Amazon while playing an ecotourism simulation game.

Jungle Photos
www.junglephotos.com
Visit this site to view hundreds of Amazon photos, from animals to children.

Skill Matching Page

What did you learn? Look at the questions in the "Skills" column. Compare them to the page number of the answers in the "Page" column. Refresh your memory by reading the "Answer" column below.

SKILLS	ANSWER	PAGE
What facts did I learn from this book?	I learned that the Amazon rain forest is the largest rain forest in the world.	4
What skills did I learn?	I learned how to read maps.	5, 7, 16–17
What activities did I do?	I answered the questions in the quiz.	28–29
How can I find out more?	I can read the books and visit the Web sites from the Find Out for Yourself page.	30
How can I get involved?	I can help save Amazonian trees by buying less mahogany wood.	24–25

Glossary

caffeine: a substance in certain plants, coffee, and tea that, when consumed, can make people lively and wide awake

carbon dioxide: a gas that is found normally in the atmosphere and is absorbed by plants

deforestation: the act of removing trees from an area

greenhouse effect: the dangerous warming of Earth

humus: a brownish, mushy substance made up of dead, decomposing parts of plants and animal waste on a forest floor

ice age: a period of time when a large area of Earth is covered by ice glaciers

indigenous: native to a certain place; having been born in a place

lasers: devices that emit a beam of radiation

latex: a liquid produced by certain types of plants that is made into rubber

nutrients: any substance that provides nourishment

predators: animals that hunt and kill other animals for food

satellite: a spacecraft that travels around Earth and transmits communication signals

species: a specific group of plant or animal that shares characteristics

tributaries: bodies of water that feed into larger bodies of water, such as rivers

Index